Buddhist Pilgrimage

ISBN: 0-89346-917-3

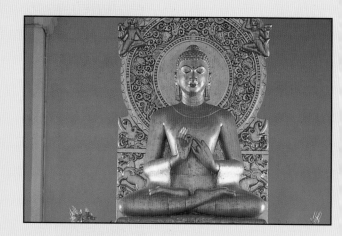

Buddhist Pilgrimage

Text: BRIJ TANKHA

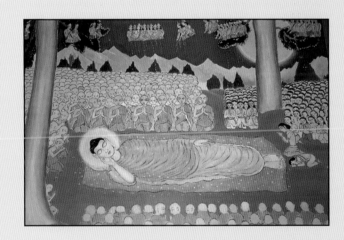

HEIAN INTERNATIONAL INC.

1815 West 205th Street, Suite #301
Torrance, CA 90501

310 - 328 - 7200

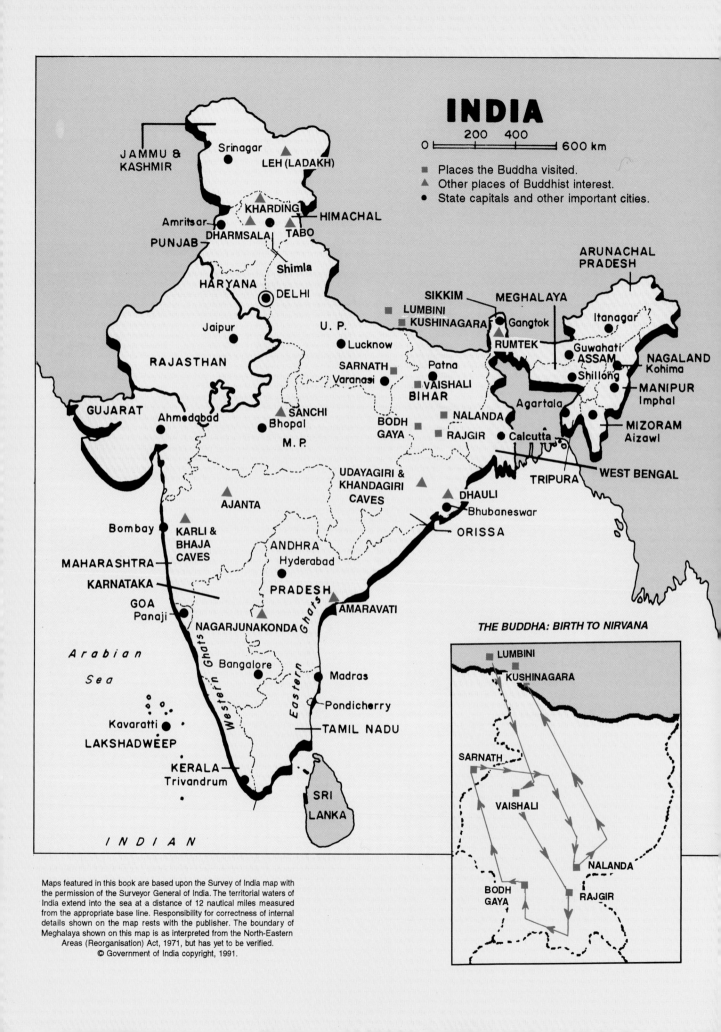

INDIA

0   200   400   600 km

■ Places the Buddha visited.
▲ Other places of Buddhist interest.
● State capitals and other important cities.

JAMMU & KASHMIR
Srinagar
LEH (LADAKH)
KHARDING
Amritsar
DHARMSALA
HIMACHAL
TABO
PUNJAB
Shimla
HARYANA
DELHI
Jaipur
U. P.
Lucknow
RAJASTHAN
LUMBINI
KUSHINAGARA
SIKKIM
MEGHALAYA
Gangtok
RUMTEK
ARUNACHAL PRADESH
Itanagar
Guwahati
ASSAM
NAGALAND
Kohima
Shillong
MANIPUR
Imphal
SARNATH
Varanasi
Patna
VAISHALI
BIHAR
SANCHI
Bhopal
M. P.
BODH GAYA
NALANDA
RAJGIR
Agartala
Calcutta
MIZORAM
Aizawl
GUJARAT
Ahmedabad
TRIPURA
WEST BENGAL
UDAYAGIRI & KHANDAGIRI CAVES
DHAULI
Bhubaneswar
ORISSA
AJANTA
KARLI & BHAJA CAVES
Bombay
MAHARASHTRA
KARNATAKA
ANDHRA
Hyderabad
PRADESH
AMARAVATI
GOA
Panaji
NAGARJUNAKONDA
Western Ghats
Eastern Ghats
Bangalore
Madras
Pondicherry
TAMIL NADU
Arabian Sea
Kavaratti
LAKSHADWEEP
KERALA
Trivandrum
SRI LANKA
INDIAN

THE BUDDHA: BIRTH TO NIRVANA

LUMBINI
KUSHINAGARA
SARNATH
VAISHALI
NALANDA
BODH GAYA
RAJGIR

Maps featured in this book are based upon the Survey of India map with the permission of the Surveyor General of India. The territorial waters of India extend into the sea at a distance of 12 nautical miles measured from the appropriate base line. Responsibility for correctness of internal details shown on the map rests with the publisher. The boundary of Meghalaya shown on this map is as interpreted from the North-Eastern Areas (Reorganisation) Act, 1971, but has yet to be verified.
© Government of India copyright, 1991.

The Buddha: Birth to Nirvana

Lumbini: in Nepal, the birthplace of the Buddha, born to Queen Maya, who is said to have delivered standing and supporting herself

Ruins from present-day Lumbini.

by a *sal* tree (following her dream of a white elephant entering her womb).

Kapilavastu: the modern Piprahawa, was the fortified town of Suddhodana, the father of Siddharatha (the Buddha's personal name)

Siddhartha as a young prince.

where the latter spent his youth before setting out on the way to 'Enlightenment'.

Vaishali: (located in Bihar) was the first halt for Gautama, the ascetic, once he had shed the mantle of Prince Siddharatha. He met the yoga

Ashoka Pillar in Vaishali.

teacher, Alara Kalana here. Several Ashokan Pillars are still extant here.

Rajgir: in Bihar, the capital of King Bimbisara, where Gautama met Rudraka Ramputra, a yoga master. He was to return here as the Buddha and

Buddha idol in Rajgir.

Bimbisara to become his disciple and patron. The king's conversion took place at the present location of the 'Hill of Vultures'.

Bodh Gaya: a village of Bihar is the site of 'Enlightenment' with the great *bodhi* tree under which Gautama was supposed to have meditated

Temple interior at Bodh Gaya.

and been transformed into 'the Buddha'. This spot is today marked with a red sandstone slab.

Sarnath: near Varanasi in Uttar Pradesh was where the Buddha gave his 'First Sermon'. It is said the Wheel of Law was turned here. The

Kaalchakra festival at Sarnath.

Dhamek Stupa, an imposing monument existing to date, was the site of the first sermon.

Nalanda: (in Bihar) where the Buddha preached and the monastic movement gained ground after the teacher's death. It emerged as a great university

Remains of Nalanda Vihar.

around the 4th-5th century AD. There remain parts of around 11 monasteries even today.

Kushinagara: (also, Kushinara) in Nepal, is the region where the Buddha died (in a *sal* grove) — and is said to have attained *Mahaparinibbana,*

The Great Decease, Kushinagara.

salvational bliss upon death/cessation of being. The Nirvana stupa here dates from Ashoka's time.

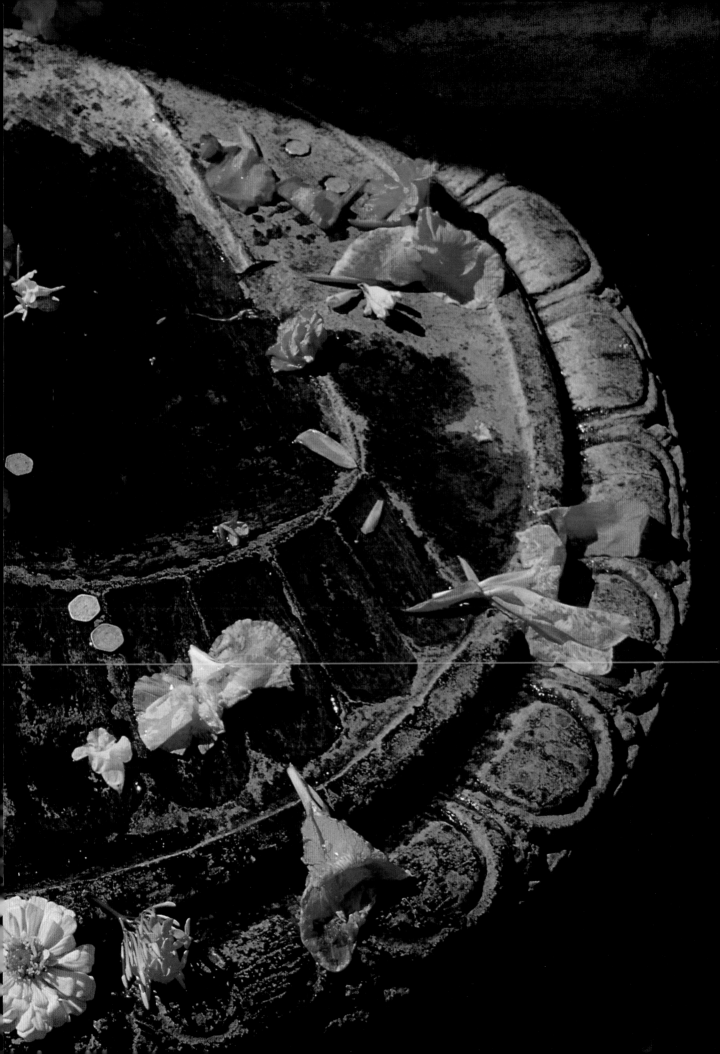

Preceding pages
6-7: *In the temple enclosure of Bodh Gaya, the place of 'Enlightenment', on a large, carved stone is incised the Buddha's* caranas *(footprints). Pilgrims sprinkle water here and adorn these footprints with flowers. The stone itself is bordered with rose-lotus leaves.*

Pages 8-9: *A huge congregation of Lamaistic Buddhist monks during the Kaalchakra festival, an occasion of initiation for young monks, especially. The Dalai Lama is at the head of this ceremony. 'Kaalchakra' literally means 'the wheel of time'.*

This page:
Young monk in a Nepalese monastery with a panel covered with Buddha icons. In the present-day Nepal is located Lumbini, where the Buddha was born to Queen Maya of the Sakya dynasty. Lumbini's (Nepal's as well, in general) interest as a pilgrimage is inseperable from the sanctification associated with the Buddha's birth.

***Following pages
12-13:*** *Wall painting from Moolgandh Kuti, Sarnath. It represents the* Jataka *tale of a grieving mother who once brought to the Buddha her dead child beseeching him to restore it to life. The Buddha asked her to get some mustard seeds from a household where no death has been experienced. And the child would be saved. The mother went on this impossible search. After some time she returned, having learnt to cope with her bereavement through this lesson in compassion.*

Pages 14-15: *A monk's sombre welcoming of the rising sun at Vaishali, where the Buddha preached his last sermon. Vaishali was visited by the famous Chinese travellers Fa Hsien and Hiuen Tsang, who is to known to have taken a piece of sculpture from one of the* stupas *here.*

Introduction

And the end of all our exploring
Will be to arrive where we started
And know the place for the first time.

—T. S. Eliot

A pilgrimage is an adventure in time and place, it is a recapitulation as well as a rediscovery; a journey both outward and inward. A journey to the sites associated with the Buddha is an occasion to consider his quest for knowledge and the larger intellectual ferment of that exciting and creative period. And out of the interaction of this ferment and the Buddha's personal 'Enlightenment' is forged what later generations will recognise as 'Buddhism'.

The key places of the Buddha's life—his 'stations' as it were—are sites of civilizational significance. They are monuments, even if in a present state of physical decay, to the spiritual heritage of what self-evidently appears today as 'modern India'. Buddhism, an accepted religion among the many which exist in modern India, was, in reality, a gradual formation created partly out pre-existent teachings, for example, those of Makkhali Gosala and Purana Kassapa and eventually Buddhist teaching flowed over across the Indian frontiers.

Thus the occasion is also one to reflect on the manner in which the message of the Buddha spread, binding large parts of Asia, on how Buddhism became a carrier of a range of ideas and practices which have become integral to the civilizations of Asia.

The 6th century BC was a period when northern India witnessed profound intellectual activity. New philosophical concepts, religious sects which questioned accepted ideas and changes in the social and economic conditions of society were the hallmarks of this period. The Buddha's ideas, then, are not examples of isolated brilliance, and rather derived their strength from the prevailing community of ideas.

The details of the actual life of the Buddha are largely a matter of conjecture. Some texts, notably the *Sutta Nipata*, mention some biographical details but most tracts were written at a considerably later date when the process of deification was gaining in intensity. Broadly speaking, there are four types of interpretation of the Buddha's life. First, there is a certain scholarship which points out that for 'the Perfected Man', the sequence of birth, suffering, death have no relevance. Next, some commentators have drawn attention to the life of the Buddha in terms of an allegorical illustration of the philosophical principles of the Samkhya School. Thirdly, some have favoured a mystic interpretation bringing into correlation some archetypal solar myths and the Buddha's life. And finally, it has been proposed that the historical Buddha is of no importance—the Buddha is essentially an 'idea' which manifests itself in different periods, through different personalities.

The paucity of historical information regarding the actual circumstances of the Buddha's life and the frequent dismissal of stories associated with him as fanciful make a historical re-creation particularly difficult. Even the name by which he is known, that is 'Buddha', is merely a generic name implying a superior being: superior because of his knowledge of the 'Truth'. He was generally referred to as *Tathagata* after he attained 'Enlightenment'. His personal name was Siddharatha and his *gotra* (lineage, to admit a free translation) name, Gautama. He has also been addressed as Sakka, Brahma, Mahamuni and Yakkha.

The Buddha delivered his discourses in the dialects of Magadha and Kosal rather than in Sanskrit, the language of the literati.

Facing page: A Buddhist acolyte, spending his early monkhood persuing the scriptures.

His insistence that the language of the region be used has meant that the Buddhist Canon has come down to us in many languages. The Pali Canon, for instance, is said to refer to the version written in Ceylon but which originated in India. (Pali literally means a line of a sacred text, and is not the name of language.)

The older texts of Buddhism are not written as biographies of the Buddha, though some scholars do talk of a biography composed about a hundred years after the Buddha's death. There are stray references and the occasional mention of some detail of the Buddha's life, and these deal mainly with the person after his renunciation. However, in Sanskrit sources, such as the *Lalitavistara* (The Pleasurable Biography) and the *Divyavadana* (The Divine Adventure), the Buddha's life is traced from pre-births upto his *parinibbana* or death. These earlier writings laid emphasis on the Buddha's teachings and it is only later that other authors attempted to reconstruct his life and the sequence of his teaching.

The most famous early biography was composed by Asvaghosa, sometime between the 1st and 2nd century AD. Originally it consisted of twenty-eight cantos in Sanskrit, of which only seventeen survive, which reflect the devotional aspect of Buddhism. *Buddha Charita* (Life of the Buddha) by Asvaghosa was a sensual potrayal of the early life of the Buddha and though its main purpose was didactic, illustrating the teachings of the Buddha, Asvaghosa created a fine work of art transmuting history into legend and life into art.

The Chinese traveller I-Ching, who came to India in AD 645 wrote about the *Buddha Charita* that it is, 'widely read or sung throughout the five divisions of India and the countries of the Southern Sea. He [Asvaghosa] clothes the manifold meanings and ideas in a few words which rejoice the heart of the reader so that he never feels tired of reading the poem. Besides,

it should be counted as meritorious for one to read this book, in so much as it contains the noble doctrine given in a concise form.'

Though the existence of the Buddha is not a matter of controversy, dates relating to his life are still subject to debate. Based on the Ceylon chronicles, BC 563-483 is generally considered to be an acceptable life-span. He was born in Lumbini, in the Sakya clan (Sakya in Buddhist texts is connected to the oak tree and in others it refers to one who has power) and at the age of twenty-nine he left his family and residence to lead a homeless life. At thirty-five, at Bodh Gaya, he attained 'Enlightenment', and at the age of eighty he died at Kushinagara. His teachings found adherents in and around the kingdoms of Magadha and Kosala (south Bihar and eastern Uttar Pradesh) and their neighbourhood. The Buddha established a community of monks which was called *Sangha*. Together with the Buddha and the doctrine, *dhamma*, *Sangha* forms the three tenets in which the believer seeks refuge. Buddhism gave an important place to the deity and, in general, welcomed all classes of society into its fold. The select band of monks who formed the *Sangha* made possible the continuation of Buddhism after the passing away of the Buddha.

Around the time of the birth of the Buddha, political conditions in northern India were going through a process of change and restructuring. There were sixteen major states contending for power and hegemony. Broadly speaking, the political units were divided into monarchies, like Kosala and Magadha and oligarchies like the Sakya, the Malla and the Vajji. (Though the Sakyas were not one of the sixteen major states of the time.) The monarchies were located in the Ganga-Jamuna valley while the oligarchies were mostly in the Himalayan foothills. These were territorial units with complex administrative and political structures and growing into powerful economies.

The oligarchies were organised around clans and were faced with the task of defending themselves against the expanding monarchies. Alive to this threat, they often attempted to form alliances with each other to fight off this challenge. They were however, unable to stem the inexorable growth of the kingdoms of Magadha, Kosala, Vatsa and Avanti. The Sakyas came, it is believed, from central India to the Himalayan foothills around the time of the birth of the Buddha. Buddha's father, Suddhodana was said to be the head of a clan of five-hundred families. The clan was based in the fortified town of Kapilavastu. The Sakyas nominally acknowledged allegiance to the kingdom of Kosala which lay to the southwest of the Sakya territory. The Sakyas are described as proud and noble *khattiyas* (an Aryan warrior class) but some of their practices, such as inter-marriage between close relatives, suggest non-Aryan influences. Widespread colonisation had been made possible with the discovery of iron ore and the development of technological skills to carbonize and strengthen it. Iron ore had been discovered earlier in other parts of the subcontinent but in the Ganga-Jamuna region it was discovered around this period and this allowed for large scale clearing of forests. The spread of rice cultivation and greater productivity made it possible to support larger populations and people gathered in cities where they turned to occupations other than agriculture. As the historian, A. L. Basham writes, 'In the cities, men of many tribes rubbed shoulders together, uprooted from their lands and separated from their own clansmen. In most parts of the Ganga valley, ambitious kings had virtually eliminated the tribal institutions which had prevailed in earlier times. New groups of merchants and skilled craftsmen were gaining in wealth and influence.'

Parallel with the economic changes was a ferment in the realm of ideas. A range of philosophies from fatalism to materialism flourished. Long held beliefs and practices came under scrutiny and questioning. In particular, the special claim of the Brahmana to knowledge came under attack. The *sramanas*, who were homeless wanderers challenged the primacy of Vedic practices. The Buddha too, initially appeared to the people as a destroyer of homes. However, by rejecting the extremes of ascetic discipline, the Buddha forged links with his lay followers and created a wide circle of adherents around a nucleus of the ordained.

As the *bikkhuni* (or nun), Kundala Kesi said, 'I am living on the alms of the people but I owe no debt for I preach the *dhamma* to the people in the realm.'

In the Buddhist conception, *dana* (charity) began to occupy the place formerly reserved for sacrifice in Vedic rituals. Charity provided a means for the lay person to acquire merit. However, unlike earlier gifts of land to individuals, in Buddhism land was given to the *Sangha* and not to an individual monk.

The acceptance of land first arose because the monks used to spend the rainy season in one place, their *vassavasa*. It is said that the king of Magadha, Bimbisara thought, 'There is *veluvanna*, my pleasure garden, which is not too far from the town and not too near. What if I were to make an offering of the *veluvanna* to the fraternity of the *bikkhus* with the venerable Buddha at its head.' This first gift was accepted by the Buddha for the *Sangha*. It is worth bearing in mind that the gifts were never of agricultural land. Nevertheless the very acceptance of gifts created a debate with some monks arguing that this was a dilution of monastic discipline.

Buddhist ideas can be categorised within the marginal stream called *sramana*. The *sramanas* were those who had rejected worldly life and withdrawn into the forests to live a life of renunciation. The Brahmana sects were *astika* because they

accepted the Vedas as the supreme authority and their goals were fundamentally of men pursuing aims in accordance with the moral law (*dharma* or *rita*). For the *sramanas*, however, *karma* or action became an important idea, the moral consequences of actions being unavoidable.

The Buddha was not alone in criticising the Vedic emphasis on sacrifice and ritual. The Upanishads had first pointed out the way of knowledge and meditation as a path to liberation. Unlike the Upanishads, however, the Buddha did not engage in abstruse philosophising, dismissing it as mere intellectual jugglery.

The Buddhist doctrine saw everyone as having an equal chance to achieve salvation. The Buddha ordained men from all walks of life—fishermen, potters, barbers . . . however, women were considered inferior since, as women they could not attain salvation and it was only with reluctance that they were admitted to the *Sangha*. Initially slaves were allowed to become monks but later they first had to be freed by their masters before being admitted into the *Sangha*. Of all the sects then, only the *Ajivikas* treated the slaves as equal, some of the latter even going on to become teachers.

Buddhism's contribution to changing unjust social practices was thus limited and several scholars are critical of this failure. It has been written that Buddhism was the 'biggest socio-religious movement in Indian history' but it only created an 'illusion of equality' in the *Sangha* even while these values were ignored in society at large.

An over-emphasis on one aspect of the Buddha's teachings may distort the rich complexity of his thought, but the dominant strain of his teachings was expressed with striking simplicity to his favourite disciple, Ananda: 'And whosoever, Ananda, either now or after I am dead, shall be a lamp unto themselves, and a refuge unto themselves, shall betake themselves to no external refuge, but holding fast to the 'Truth' as their camp, not look for refuge to anyone besides themselves, it is they . . . who shall reach the very top-most height. But they must be anxious to learn.'

This 'anxiety to learn' truly motivated Siddharatha to leave the comfort of home and family and search for the meaning of life. The basic belief that the path to righteousness could be gained by knowledge and effort: a path open to all (though in practice largely to men) and not dependent on the seeker's status, arises from this starting point. The Buddha's quest thus leads him to greater knowledge which in turn deepens his understanding and compassion. The appeal of his message across centuries and across continents lies surely in this compassion.

Facing page: *The great miracle of Sravasti, depicted at the Ajanta caves, one in which the Buddha created a 'thousand' images of himself in the air. These images, self-identical, were a response to the provocation by six sects and their leaders.*

Where the Buddha was Born

Where is the Prince, I want to see him?

—Asita, Sutta Nipata

'On the last day of *Asada* (June-July) on the moon festival day, Mayadevi dreams that the Bodhisattva who was roaming in the Himalayas in the form of a white elephant, descends from the north, on the silver mountain and enters her womb from the right side. Thus on Lunar *Uttarasal* she receives a new conception.' Asvaghosa, in his biography, adds to this description that 'before conceiving the Queen saw in her dream a six-tusked, white, god-like elephant entering her body, and yet she felt no pain.'

The future Buddha was born in Lumbini Garden (in the present day Basti district of Nepal), between the territory of the Sakyas and the Koliyas. His mother Queen Maya, on her way to her family home at Devadha, the capital of the Koliya, stopped for a while at Lumbini. It was as she was plucking flowers from the *asoka* tree that she felt the beginnings of labour. The story handed down by tradition is that she delivered Siddharatha while standing, supporting herself by holding a *sal* tree. In Sanchi, a panel on the first gateway, depicts this auspicious scene of the Buddha's birth: 'Being entreated by the

The northern gate among the famous gateways at Sanchi, called toranas. *The architecture here consists of two pillars joined by three archi-traves (cross beams) built as if they actually passed through the upright posts. The carvings on these gateways represent the Buddha's life, scenes from* Jataka *stories and legends associated with the Buddha's previous lives.*

23

A mural typical of the last Ajanta period (6th-7th century). It depicts the birth of the future Buddha in Lumbini. The female figures are 'stylized' and expressions 'theatrical'.

gods of the *Tushita* heaven, Bodhisattva descended to the earth in the form of a white elephant.' This elephant spoken of denotes power and wisdom.

Lumbini became a pilgrimage site very early. In BC 250, it is said, the Emperor Ashoka along with his teacher Upagupta visited the place during a tour of Buddhist sites. While there, he had a pillar and a stone wall built to mark his visit. Later visitors, particularly the Chinese travellers Fa Hsien in the fifth and Hiuen Tsang in the seventh centuries mention a beautiful grove and describe a bathing tank of the Sakyas. The travellers also write of the *asoka* tree where the Buddha was born, but the Ashokan pillar and wall were, according to their accounts, already dilapidated and broken

Facing page: *From the Ajanta paintings of Cave no. 2, this is the Bodhisattva enthroned in the heaven of the Thirty-three Gods, where he waits to descend to earth in his final human form. He is dressed in princely garb and makes the gesture of instruction.*

with age. Hiuen Tsang writes that they were ruined not by age but by the thunderbolt of a malicious dragon.

After the visits of these early travellers, Lumbini slumbered in dusty obscurity till 1895 when the German archaeologist, Dr Alois Anton Fuhrer re-discovered the site. The Ashokan pillar was unearthed the following year and on it was found an inscription recording the visit of the Emperor Ashoka: 'Because the Lord Buddha was born here, he made the village of Lumbini free from taxes and subject to pay only one-eighth of the produce as land revenue instead of the usual rate.'

However, the location of Kapilavastu, the fortified town of the Buddha's father Suddhodana, was more difficult to identify. Some scholars have agreed that it is the present day Tilwara Kot in Nepal while others have claimed that it is modern Piprahawa in India. Both these places are close to Lumbini Garden and some scholars, trying to reconcile the

Queen Maya, mother of the future Buddha, depicted in Ajanta (cave no. 2). Maya, wife of Suddhodana, the king of Kapilavastu was supposed to have died and gone to heaven immediately after giving birth.

conflict, state that both were the site of Kapilavastu at different times.

Early excavations at Piprahawa unearthed various artifacts, among which was a soapstone casket with the inscription: 'This relic shrine of the divine Buddha is a donation of the Sakya Sukiti brothers associated with their sisters, sons, and wives.' This strengthened Piprahawa's claim to be the site of Kapilavastu and the claim was further advanced when excavations carried out by K. M. Srivastava for the Archaeological Survey of India in 1971 and 1974 yielded other artifacts.

To the devoted, more than the sites, it is the birth of the Buddha which is an opening act in the realisation of an idea: knowledge based on compassion. In later traditions the Buddha

Facing page: Lumbini. In this relief (7th century) of the birth of the future Buddha, the old sage Asita establishes the presence on the child's body of the thirty-two signs of holiness. Below, a haloed Siddhartha takes his first steps.

already enfolds in himself all the attributes that he will eventually acquire and the birth scene is filled with signs signifying the future greatness of the child. The mother, Queen Maya is reported to have died within seven days of the birth of the child. Tradition passes on the statement that, 'she who bears a Peerless One like me should not again indulge in love.' Asvaghosa dealt with the scene more poetically, writing, 'when Queen Maya saw the vast power of her son, like that of a divine seer, she was unable to bear the joy it caused her. Then she went to heaven to dwell there.' Later, in the finely sculpted gateway at Sanchi, a celestial ladder is shown with footprints above and below the ladder to signify the descending of the Bodhisattva.

The miraculous birth was followed by a bath given by the *nagas* (creatures said to be half human, half snakes) and tradition has it thus: 'Just born, the Bodhisattva stands firmly on his feet and takes seven steps, his face towards the

27

north. Shaded by the white parasol, he looks to each cardinal point and speaks the following words in stentorian tones (like the roar of a lion), "I am the first, I am the best of all beings." He then proceeds to take a step in each direction and in each direction he utters an appropriate word suggesting that the beneficent rain of his Law would now shower on all the people—the good and the bad.'

The newly born child was taken to his father Suddhodana at Kapilavastu. At the court, the sage Asita prophesied the future greatness of the child: 'For my time to depart has come, just when he is born who shall understand the means, so hard to find, of destroying birth. For he will give up the kingdom in his indifference to worldly pleasures, and, through bitter struggles grasping the final truth, he will shine forth as a sun of knowledge in the world to dispel the darkness of delusion.'

Suddhodana on hearing this promise of greatness named his son Siddharatha, 'he who has accomplished his aim'. The future greatness of Siddharatha was ensured; if he carried out his kingly duties he would become the *Chakravartin Raja*, a universal monarch but even if he chose to give up his power he would emerge as a great teacher, a *Tathagata*. *Chakravartin Raja* or *Tathagata*, Siddharatha had an exceptional destiny to fulfill. It is, of course, not possible to be sure of his personal name and actually the early texts do not mention Siddharatha.

In stories culled from later traditions, the early life of Siddharatha is depicted as a moral evolution, a gradual unfolding of knowledge leading to the quest for supreme 'Enlightenment'. With his mother dead, Siddharatha was cared for by his maternal aunt, Mahaprajapati Gotami, who became his father's second wife. Siddharatha, the young prince, spent his youth in comfort and luxury: 'I was delicately nurtured. In my father's house, lotus pools of blue, red and white lotuses were made for me; I used sandalwood powder from Kasi; Kasi cloth turban, jacket, tunic and cloak. I had three palaces, one for winter, one for summer and one for the rainy season. Three palaces to gratify the five senses.'

Siddhartha's education was that of a noble of those times. It is reported that when the Emperor Ashoka visited Kapilavastu he was shown a schoolroom and a gymnasium. 'It is here, O Great King, that the Buddha learnt to write, and here that he became an expert, as suited to his noble birth, in the art of handling elephants, horses, chariots and the use of arms, etc.' Siddhartha was educated, befittingly, both in the literary and in the martial arts. The Sakyas were particularly noted for their excellence in archery and Siddhartha was reputed to be skilled in this, as he was also in every other field.

In his nineteenth year Siddharatha was married to his cousin Yasodhara, daughter of Dandapani Sakya. It is said that when he presented a costly necklace to Yasodhara she declined to accept it and said, 'No, our aim is not to despoil the prince of his ornaments, but rather to become an adornment to him.' The poet Asvaghosa merely mentions that Yasodhara was 'virtuous and endowed with beauty and gentle bearing.' They had one son, Rahula.

Even in the midst of luxury and a sheltered life, Siddharatha is shown to have had a keen sense of life's meaning. The first note of his later preoccupation was sounded at the scene of the symbolic ploughing of the fields. The feast of sowing is being celebrated and Suddhodana has the child Siddharatha brought out. However, his attendants leave him unattended under the shade of a tree, for they, too, are busy watching the symbolic ploughing in which the Sakya chief ploughs with a gold-ornamented plough. Siddharatha, under the shade of the tree, sits in a yogic posture and attains the first of the four degrees of meditation, these degrees actualized along the way to the Buddha's 'Enlightenment'. In later life he narrates this incident to his disciple Agivssena, 'I know that while my Sakyan father was ploughing and I was sitting in the cool shade of a rose apple tree, aloof from

Facing page: *Worshipping the* bodhi *tree, part of a panel from the main gateway at Sanchi, 1st century BC. The complete panel is generally entitled as 'Indra's visiting the Buddha'.*

the pleasures of the senses, aloof from the unskilled states of mind, entering on the first meditation, which is accompanied by initial thought, is born of aloofness and is rapturous, and joyful, and while abiding therein, I thought, could this be the way to awakening? Then following any mindfulness, Agvissena, there was the consciousness: this itself is the way of awakening . . .'

This incident, referred to as the 'First Meditation', shows symbolically, that this first encounter of Siddharatha was inextricably and peculiarly linked with agriculture. It was as if far removed from the material cares of the world, Siddharatha, seeing this process of growth and decay, of creation, begins to think and meditate.

The second major experience which dramatically changed Siddharatha's life was the confrontation with the fundamental questions of human existence: old age, illness and death. These are presented as four signs which Siddharatha sees—an old man, a sick man, a corpse and finally a monk. Upon this, he was compelled to consider the meaning of his life and question his worldly obligations. Everything is subject to decay and death: life is transient but the monk shows him a way out of this bondage. Siddharatha resolved to renounce the life of the householder and seek a way out of this cycle of birth and decay and find true happiness.

The second sign appeared when Siddhartha, leaving by the south gate of the city, sees 'a diseased man, dried up, overcome with fever, weak, with his body immersed in his own filth, helpless and protectorless, and breathing with difficulty.' Sickness too, it struck him, was an inevitable and inescapable fact of human existence. He saw a corpse when leaving the city by the west gate, and around it, wailing, sorrowful and disconsolate relatives. Asvaghosa writes that Siddhartha was so disconsolate that even the efforts of the women in his palace failed to distract him from the inevitability of death.

'Yes, father, I do see affliction of the body. Disease close upon health and death upon life. And father, I consider an old man as but another dead man. Death comes on father, it is this affliction of the physical body I see. Yes father, I see the decay of wealth. Everything is empty, void, vain, deceptive and false.'

It was the fourth sign which showed the way out of this dilemma, a way to resolve this crisis faced by Siddhartha. While riding his favourite horse Kanthaka, Siddhartha came upon a *sramana*, a homeless wanderer who tells him, 'I dwell wherever I happen to be, at the base of a tree or in a deserted temple, or on a hill or in the forest, and I wander without ties or expectations, in search of the highest goals, accepting any alms I receive.'

Siddhartha then became aware not only of the fleeting nature of life, the continuous cycle of creation and destruction but also of a possible way out of this incessant cycle. He became aware that not everything was transient, that there were permanent goals to which he could aspire to.

While Siddhartha was growing weary of the world and preparing to leave home, his father Suddhodana was making preparations to hand over the affairs of government to his son and heir. To further reinforce his ties to his home and family, his wife conceived.

'It is a letter which has come to me,' he is supposed to have said, though some writers are of the opinion that Rahula, meaning 'bond', had already been born.

In later accounts, dramatic scenes of Suddhodana eloquently pleading with his son not to renounce family and home, not to abandon his worldly duties, are depicted. Siddhartha remained gently adamant. His father, he argued, could not give him freedom from old age, sickness and death. He remained firm in his resolve to go and seek the answers to these questions. Suddhodana was finally persuaded to give his reluctant consent.

Siddhartha before leaving went to see his son but dared not touch him . . . 'If I lift the Queen's hand to take my son in my arms she will awake and thus my departure will be hampered. When I shall become the Buddha I will come back and see him.' He left his wife and son sleeping undisturbed.

Remains of the Buddhavihar in Lumbini—the place of the Buddha's birth. Lumbini, just 130 km across the Nepal border with India, a place of inaugural Buddhist significance and strewn with restful ruins, attracts to date pilgrims and tourists.

Siddharatha was accompanied by his groom Chandaka and his horse Kanthaka. In later writings it appears that both attempted to make him abandon his plans, but convinced by his irrefutable arguments, they eventually helped him to leave. The 'Great Departure' is garnished with all the requisite miraculous happenings: the gods put the inhabitants of Kapilavastu into a deep slumber, the hooves of Kanthaka were silenced, and the gates of the city opened on their own accord, allowing Siddhartha to leave quietly and undisturbed.

The next morning found them some distance from Kapilavastu and after crossing the Anoma river, Siddhartha removed his rich garments and exchanged them for the torn clothes of a passing hunter and then cut off his hair. Siddhartha, the Prince was thus transformed physically into a mendicant and his favourite horse, witnessing this sacrifice, 'kneeling on his forelegs licked (his master's) feet with his tongue and dropped hot tears.'

Siddhartha sent a reluctant groom and the horse back to Kapilavastu. The city despaired at his disappearance. They were pacified by the groom but on hearing that Siddhartha had taken to the 'homeless state' there was great lamentation. Kanthaka was so aggrieved that he died heartbroken.

Siddhartha proceeded southward to the kingdom of Magadha, then ruled by Bimbisara. The journey was both physical, taking him away from his home, the small Sakya state, towards the flourishing monarchy of Magadha, as well as one which was intellectual, as it set in motion, events that would transform the young Prince Siddhartha into the *Tathagata*.

Where the Buddha Received Enlightenment

When body and mind are pure,
thought is firm.
When one obtains (firm) thought,
he becomes free from all bonds.

—Chandogaya Upanishad

The first step on the road to 'Enlightenment' was the transformation of the young Prince into Gautama, the ascetic: a transformation effected when Siddhartha changed his royal robes and rich ornaments for the old and tattered clothes of a passing hunter and cut off his hair to show that he had become a *sramana*. The 'feast of the hair' is a popular motif in Buddhist sculpture though the artists of the Gandhara school ignore this motif and continue to show the Buddha with hair.

Gautama proceeded towards the city of Vaishali which was then the capital of the powerful republic of the Licchavis, one of the important members of the Vajjan confederacy, a political confederation of eight members. Gautama stopped briefly to consult some learned teachers and then proceeded to Rajagriha (Rajgir, east of present day Patna) the capital of the Magadhan monarchy. From here he went to Gaya. This seven year period is traditionally divided into two unequal parts: the first during which Gautama practised various austerities and the second, at the end of which he attained 'Enlightenment'.

Wall painting from Sarnath, in which the Buddha is in the reclining posture of the Great Decease, Mahaparinibbana. *He has his favourite diciple Ananda in attendance and the gods are shown showering flower petals.*

33

At Vaishali, Gautama met the yoga teacher Alara Kalana (Arada Kalpa) who taught the doctrine of the non-existence of all things. This did not appeal to Gautama and his stay here was brief. He then set out to meet the learned teacher Pudraka in Rajagriha (Rajgir). Rajgriha, the capital of Magadha, was ruled by King Bimbisara who became an important patron of the Buddha and because of this, later accounts talk of a meeting between the two while Gautama was still an unknown mendicant.

Gautama's study with Rudraka Ramaputra, another yoga master, proved equally unsatisfying, for he found in the attainment of yogic states neither an end to the problem of the transience of life nor the attainment of peace and true knowledge. By this time he had decided to set out on his own. Accompanied by his five companions he proceeded towards Gaya. At the village of Urubilva (modern Uruvela), which according to Chinese sources was a Brahman village in the valley of the river Nairanjana, he was reportedly charmed by the idyllic beauty of the place: its woods, water and its quiet. He stayed here for six years to undergo a series of austere practices to weaken the power of his physical body and thereby release his spirit. The 'homeless ones' found in the practice of mortifying the flesh and in a disengagement with the world a means to spiritual liberation.

Gautama initially sat immobile. He appeared to be dead and later tradition has it that the gods were worried and in despair sent Queen Maya to persuade Gautama to end these penances. But Gautama began an extraordinary regime of fasting, eating one grain of rice a day and finally, he gave up even this. His body was reduced to a mere skeleton. The *Lalitavistara* says that 'his limbs became like knotty sticks, his spine like the rough weave of a braid, his protruding thorax the ribbed shell of a crab, his head like an unripe gourd and his eyes like the reflection of stars at the bottom of a nearly dried up well. It is said that the children who saw him '. . . took him for a dust demon and made fun of him'. Yet the extreme mortification of the flesh did not produce any spiritual

awakening and Gautama was still without any answers to his questions. Here he began to perceive the futility, we are told, of ascetic practice. His thoughts went back to the 'First Meditation': salvation can only be achieved by using the faculty of reason. He then took a momentous decision. He broke his fast. The step was drastic because his five disciples saw it as a defeat, as surrender. To them Gautama, the ascetic had not been capable of discovering a noble doctrine superior to the current ethic. How could he do so now—now that he was eating food and living normally? He is nothing but a fool and an imbecile. With such thoughts, they left him.

Abandoned, Gautama set about clothing and feeding himself. From a nearby cremation ground he retrieved the shroud of a woman and, after purifying it, wore it in the manner of a robed monk. (The Chinese traveller Hiuen Tsang describes the scene, having seen the pond and the stone where Gautama washed the shroud.) Sujata, the daughter of a village headman living nearby cooked him some rice. Some writers elaborate the story, saying that she used the cream of a thousand cows and offered it to him in a golden bowl. Gautama bathed away the accumulated dirt and then sat down to eat the meal. His hair was miraculously restored. The meal over, he threw the golden bowl away and the gods instantly appeared to carry it away.

Gautama, washed and fed, was again transformed: he was now on the final road to 'Enlightenment'. From Gautama, the ascetic emerged the *Tathagata*. He left his refuge and went some six miles away toward an *aswattha* tree. While on his way there he came across the grass-cutter Savastka from whom he took a handful of grass to sit on. He reached the tree,

Facing page: Sarnath wall painting. Sujata, a milkmaid, brought to the meditating Siddhartha a bowl of milk. This nourishment sustained the prince when he was practising austerities.
Following pages 36-37: The veneration of the Vajranna, *the Diamond Seat (in Sanskrit,* vajrasana) at Bodh Gaya, where the Buddha sat in meditation and received 'Enlightenment'. Vajranna *literally means, unshakeable or indestructible.*

The Mahabodhi Temple at Bodh Gaya, which came up in the 2nd century at the site of an initial shrine set up by King Ashoka near the bodhi *tree, under which the Buddha received 'Enlightenment'.*

Eastern gate of a Thai temple at Bodh Gaya. Most Buddhist shrines replicate the shape of a stupa— *receptacle of a holy shrine. This temple with gilded roof and ornate facade resembles an East Asian pagoda.*

circumambulated it from the right side seven times, and then placed the grass at the base so that he could sit on it. Later accounts, not satisfied with a bit of grass, have a slab appear—the Diamond seat, *Vajraana* (literally meaning, indestructible, unshakeable) and on this, Gautama placed the grass and sat, facing east towards the river Nairanjana which so captivated him.

'Upon this seat, though my body dry up and my skin, my bones and flesh be dissolved— without having reached "Enlightenment" no matter how long and difficult to reach, I shall not stir from this seat.' The site of 'Enlightenment', Bodh Gaya has been the object of continuous interest to the Buddhists. It is reported that Ashoka, during his pilgrimage of Buddhist sites, visited it in BC 259 and built a temple to mark his visit. The scene is depicted in the Bharhut Stupa in Madhya Pradesh. Later, sometime in the second century AD, the

Mahabodhi Temple was built and in AD 380 a gilded image of the Buddha, symbolizing his 'Enlightenment' was installed.

The *bodhi* tree under which Gautama sat was reportedly destroyed by Sasanka, the King of Bengal sometime around AD 600 but later another local ruler, Raja Purna Varma, is reported to have restored it. The Chinese traveller Hiuen Tsang has described in great detail the objects of interest in Bodh Gaya. From his description it seems that the *bodhi* tree was

Facing page: *Mahabodhi temple at Bodh Gaya, with the outer wall displaying modern additions of the Buddha icon, apart from the older ones. The new icons are clearly East Asian in style and inspiration.* ***Following pages 40-41:*** *The altar in a Buddhist shrine. Besides the image of Buddha it has on display objects used in liturgical ritual—the lamps, the incense stick holders, cups to hold consecrated water, the canopy, the conch shell, the bell, etc.*

A young monk in the foreground, standing in veneration with a series of chortens *in the back.* Chortens *are the Tibetan equivalent for a* stupa.

surrounded by a high brick wall and around it were planted many rare trees and herbs. The tree itself, he says, was much higher at the time of the Buddha but when he (that is, Hiuen Tsang) saw it, it was around fifty feet high. 'The bark,' he writes 'is of a yellowish-white colour, the leaves and twigs of a dark green.'

As Buddhism declined, Bodh Gaya fell into disrepair much as the other Buddhist sites did. A visiting Tibetan monk reported that he found only four monks in the *vihara* and later in the 16th century a Hindu *mahant* (head priest), Gosain Giri, established his *math* (centre) at Bodh Gaya. Initially the Burmese monks played a major role in restoring Bodh Gaya but later their work was taken up by Anagarika Dharmapala who helped to restore other Buddhist sites as well. In 1870, Alexander Cunningham had been excavating in this area when the *bodhi* tree fell down and he replanted the sapling to ensure its continuation.

Under this tree Gautama sat in *dhyana* (meditation) and resolved to attain 'Enlightenment': to find a way to end the suffering caused by existence. But before achieving 'Enlightenment' or *sambodhi* he had to confront and conquer the world of desire represented by 'Mara', the personification of love and death. This struggle was essential because the message of the Buddha is grounded in the suppression of desire and the annihilation of the self. Mara is the ruler of the sensual world and as that which is born must die, so Mara is also death. The temptation of Mara, whom the Buddhists referred to as *papian* (the evil one) is reminiscent of Yama, the god of death, tempting Nachiketa, a Brahman youth in the *Katha Upanishad*. Mara argues that the Buddha must preserve his health and that his physical needs must also be fulfilled. He must pursue the proper stages of life in an orderly manner: celibate seeker of truth, householder

Such rows of miniature stupas, *or* chortens *can be seen at many* vihars—*monastic compounds—marking the sites where relics of holy personages are preserved.*

performing the proper rituals and acquiring merit. The Buddhist doctrine was seen as disruptive and destructive of the social order, the structure of the family.

Before Gautama could attain 'Enlightenment' he had to repulse the forces of Mara. Mara's army of demons and monsters, cruel beasts with deformed bodies, are usually depicted attacking with their arrows and missiles but they are ineffective, the arrows are changed into flowers and 'Mara, the demon, sad, discouraged, his heart bleeding from a secret wound, reflecting as he draws lines upon the ground with an arrow: Gautama, the ascetic will destroy my empire.'

Mara tries to tempt Gautama and calls his daughters, Pleasure, Displeasure and Concupiscence who, with suggestive gestures and soft words, try and lure Gautama away from his resolved path. Gautama flutters his eyelashes and turns them back into their ugly old selves.

With the armies of desire routed, Gautama turns back to his meditation. The period from this point is traditionally divided into three watches of four hours each.

In each of these stages the Buddha achieves a higher state of knowledge: the falsity of doctrines, a panoramic view of the stages that man goes through because of his *karma* and finally the extinction of suffering. According to early texts, the Buddha struggled for seven years, pursued by Mara, to cultivate a compassionate mind. The popular view that after he left asceticism, he achieved 'Enlightenment' is misleading because the early Buddhists praised asceticism and many followed it as well. Later tradition divides the duration of Buddha's pursuit into a six-year period when he practised physical austerities and one year when he gave these up to sit and meditate under the *bodhi* tree.

The third watch brings Gautama up against the ultimate problem: the extinction of suffering.

This fresco depicts one of the fierce deities in the Buddhist pantheon. The imagery and treatment is strongly reminiscent of Tibetan thangka *paintings.*

In Buddhist literature the way in which he arrived at this is known as the 'Twelve Productions'. These start from the proposition that 'the unfortunate fact is that no recourse is to be found against this aggregate of pain, old age, illness, death and what follows. No way is known for putting an end to this great accumulation of suffering.' Gautama starts with the question of suffering and traces its roots. 'Here is suffering and here is the origin of suffering, here is the suppression of suffering,

Facing page: *A giant statue 20m tall on a 5m base, of the Buddha meditating, from Bodh Gaya. This statue is located near a modern Japanese temple with gold images of the Buddha.*
Following page 46: *A scene of pilgrimage, veneration and sermon from Rajgir in front of a contemporary Buddhist structure with a monument with Japanese inscriptions.*
Page 47: *Congregation inside a monastery at Rajgir. This is not really a pilgrims' gathering; rather a heterogenous meeting of individuals of different personal faiths.*

here is the way which leads to the suppression of suffering. All this I have come to know as it is. And that is how the Bodhisattva in the last watch of the night . . . became enlightened by the Supreme and complete "Enlightenment".'

The doctrine of the Buddha is referred to in a number of ways but one story encapsulates its essence: Sariputra, before he found refuge in the Buddha, met Asvajit and asked him about the Buddha's teachings. Asvajit replied that 'the *Tathagata* has explained the origin of those things which proceed from a cause. Their cessation too, he has explained. This is the doctrine of the great *Sramana.*'

The Buddha's 'Enlightenment' is not a solution of the mystery of the origin of the world but a recognition that the elements of human life are transient; that all combinations of these elements are themselves fleeting; that suffering is common to all. The sorrow of existence and its cessation through knowledge is the organising principle of the Buddha's discourse.

By the time it was morning, at the end of his night of meditation, Gautama, the ascetic had been transformed into the Buddha, the 'Enlightened One'. There is a debate in the founding texts of Buddhism about how long he remained in the blissful state: the period varies from seven days to seven weeks. In reference to this period, later stories attribute many acts to the Buddha. In the first week he sat under an *ajapala* tree and converted a Brahmin. In the second week he walked on a brick-paved road. This road was reportedly seen by the Chinese traveller Hiuen Tsang and the remnants dug up during excavations by Sir Alexander Cunningham. The contemplation of the *bodhi* tree by the Buddha is commemorated by the sanctuary of the 'Unblinking Look' at Bodh Gaya.

With this period is also associated a story featuring the Naga king Mucilinda (the king of Snakes). The story goes that the Buddha was lost in deep meditation. Even the incessant and heavy rain failed to disturb him. When the downpour threatened to submerge and drown the Buddha, the Naga king wound himself around the Buddha seven times and spread his great hood to protect him from the rain and cold. When the rains ended, the Naga uncoiled himself and worshipped the Buddha.

Just as Sujata had given him a meal which ended the six years of austere penances and began the new stage when he set himself firmly on the road to 'Enlightenment', so too the seven weeks after *sambhodhi* were concluded with a meal offered by two travelling merchants. The Buddha was under the *tarayana* tree when the two brothers Tapusha and Bhallika, at the head of a long caravan of merchants chanced upon him. They were on their way to the flourishing markets of Rajgir and Vaishali which were the focal points of lively trade at that time.

They came upon the Buddha just before noon, the appropriate time to offer food to a monk, and after worshipping him, offered him

honey and peeled sugarcane. The Buddha, who had thrown his golden bowl into the river, had nothing to accept the food in. Being a monk, he could not partake of it directly with his hands. Felicitously, the guardians of the Four Directions, the four cardinal points, intervened and offered golden bowls. But the Buddha rejected them. They next offered four stone bowls which the Buddha accepted. He placed the bowls, one into the other, making them one. Now he could accept the offering of the merchants and eat his first meal after 'Enlightenment'.

The scene of the four bowls being made into one is often depicted in Buddhist art. The Chinese traveller Fa Hsien wrote that he found the Buddha's bowl in Peshawar where it was an object of veneration. However, by the time of Hiuen Tsang, the monastery where this relic was kept had disappeared.

Significantly, it is from among the merchants that chanced upon him and offered him food. His message found great appeal among this class and they in turn were his greatest patrons. In return for the alms, the Buddha instructed them and also gave them his hair and nail clippings.

The Buddha had now to decide whether at all he should preach what he had discovered. This doubt arose because what he sought to preach would neither be easily understood nor widely welcomed. Later texts even have the god Brahma convincing the Buddha that he must go ahead and preach his message. One tradition says that the Buddha was ultimately convinced of the necessity of spreading his teachings when looking at a lotus pond. In the lotus flower he found an analogy for society. Just as lotus flowers are either fully immersed in water, or trying to rise above it, or, in some cases, quite fully above, so it is with human beings: some sunk in error are beyond hope; others have risen on their own and need no help; yet others, the great majority, are between error and truth and it is this group which needs help and succour. Finally convinced, the Buddha set out to spread his message. He went to Varanasi (called 'Kasi' then) where his five disciples who had abandoned him were now living.

Facing page: Two boy-monks gazing at the flickering glow of a score of lamps. This liturgical glow seems to indicate a long journey to be led of monastic contemplation and practice.
Following pages 50-51: Rajgir.

Where the Buddha turned the Wheel of Dhamma

*I go to the city of Kasi
beating the drum of deathlessness
in the world of blinding darkness*

—Majjhima Nikaya

The teachings of the Buddha have been vividly described as the 'paw of the lion' for 'what it strikes, be it lofty or low, it strikes soundly.' The teachings no doubt gained in authority with time. But in the lively intellectual atmosphere of that time when a number of philosophical schools were contending with each other for predominance, winning adherents was no simple matter. Tradition hands down this story: the Buddha, when he set out to find his five former disciples after his 'Enlightenment', encountered Upaka, an adherent of the *Ajivika* sect. 'Where are you going, revered Gautama?' asked Upaka. 'I am going to Varanasi to enlighten the blindness of the world and to set the wheel of a new law in motion.' Upaka, unmoved, replied, 'Very well, Gautama.'

Varanasi was an important commercial and intellectual centre,

The bell held in one hand of this monk symbolizes the primal sound as well as the resonating transcendent call of the dharma *(approximately, 'law') and the miniature* vajra *in the other hand is the admantine symbol signifying purity, incorruptibility.*
Following pages 54-55: *A typical scene of the Banaras ghats, one with a largely Hindu enviornment with people of this faith taking a holy bath in the river Ganga. The Buddha is considered one of the* dashavatars, *ten incarnations of Lord Vishnu, within certain sets of Hindu belief.*

The bodhi *tree at Sarnath, Banaras. This tree, under which Siddhartha is known to have become 'the Buddha', is identified generally with the* pipal *variety of trees. Its botanical appellation is* Ficius Religiosa.

although its power was on the wane. The Kosala kingdom had annexed the city. However, it remained a bone of contention between Kosala and Magadha. Bimbisara, the king of Magadha, married a daughter of the ruler of Varanasi (Kasi). Finally Ajatasatru, son of King Bimbisara, received it as a dowry from Kosala. As the historian Moti Chandra writes, 'Varanasi at this time was so celebrated that it was the only suitable place for the Buddha to teach a new way and turn the Wheel of Law.'

In Varanasi the Buddha met his former disciples but they were not easily convinced by his claim to 'Truth'. It was only after several attempts to convince them that they recognised his achievments. Later traditions show that they were so overwhelmed by the majesty of his presence that despite their resolve to ignore him, when he approached them, they rose to greet him.

Sarnath (or Isipatana) in the vicinity of Varanasi was the place where the 'First Sermon' was preached. The site of this preaching, the deer park called 'Saranganatha' derives its name from the herd of deer which was then protected by the King himself. Here, besides preaching the Law, the Buddha also established the order of monks: *Sangha*. The five disciples, who had rejected him because of his failure to carry out the demands of an ascetic discipline, were the nucleus of this *Sangha*. These five, Ajanta Kaudinya, Dhoddiya, Vappa, Mahanama and Assaji, are known as the *panchavargiya bikkhus*.

The 'middle path' which was proclaimed by the Buddha renounced both habitual devotion to the passions as well as self-mortification, which is considered painful, ignoble, unprofitable. Also known as the 'Noble Eightfold Path', it stresses learning by precepts, meditation and wisdom. Precepts are correct mental and physical habits which

The Moolgandh Kuti at Sarnath, Banaras behind which structure lies the famous deer park where the Buddha, once 'enlightened' preached for the first time. This first sermon was delivered to five Sanghas. *The Moolgandh Kuti contains frescoes by the Japanese artist Kosets Nosu depicting scenes from the Buddha's life.*

are important because all actions, good or bad have an effect. Meditation is the process by which the body and mind can be unified. Wisdom leads to correct judgement. In the unity of these three elements lies the essence of the 'Eightfold path'. Next, the Buddha elaborated the four 'Noble Truths' which define the origin and cause of suffering and its cessation: that is by following the 'middle path'.

In the text *Majjhima Nikaya* there is an aptly illustrative comment (as part of an ensuing dialogue with the Buddha): Sumakhatta, in the city of Vaishali says, 'The ascetic Gautama teaches a doctrine which is gained by logical thinking, built upon critical investigation, discovered by himself, and the object of proclaiming his doctrine is simply that, whosoever thinks logically, will arrive at a complete destruction of suffering.'

Not only was the 'Wheel of Law' turned at Sarnath, also from here was marked the continuation and propagation of his ideas. The nucleus of a *Sangha* was formed and the Buddha instructed his disciples. 'I shall go to the village of Sena. You go into various regions, as you like, but let no two of you go together. Teach and guide as many people as possible.' The Buddhist order is the oldest existing religious organization and though initially the monks were indistinguishable from other mendicants, gradually a code of discipline was evolved. The monks would assemble twice a month on days of the full moon and the new moon. The *pratmokkha* or rules which were compiled before the death of the Buddha were recited at these assemblies. Later, an order of nuns was also established.

King Ashoka, a devout Buddhist pilgrim

Head Monk of a Tibetan monastery at Sarnath, preparing the ritual 'scene'—he is pouring oil into the lamp, which will then be lit up as part of ritual worship.

came to Sarnath and had two stupas erected (Dharmarajika and Dhamek) as well as a monolith pillar with a lion capital and crowned with a *dharmachakra* or wheel of Law. Later Chinese travellers, who are an important source for the description of the Buddhist sites, describe the buildings, which were later ravaged in the 11th century and subsequently declined into desuetude. In 1794, the Diwan of Banaras (or Varanasi) used the Dharmarajika Stupa for building material and the relics of the Buddha were reportedly thrown away. It was the reports of the Commissioner of Banaras, Mr Jonathan Duncan, in the Asiatic Researches, which rekindled an interest in this site. Later excavations by Alexander Cunningham led to the discovery of a relic casket and subsequently F. C. Hartel uncovered the Ashoka pillar as well as an image of the Buddha delivering his 'First Sermon'.

The Buddha proceeded from Sarnath to Uruvela where the three Kashyapa brothers lived in their hermitage. On his way he met a group of young men looking for a courtesan who had stolen some of their valuables. When they asked the Buddha whether he had seen the courtesan, the Buddha deflected the question and asked the young men whether it would not be better to 'look for themselves'. Struck by this unexpected answer in the form of a question, they instantly became his disciples. This brief and suggestive story indicates the

Facing page: *This is the imposing Dhamek Stupa at Sarnath during the Kaalchakra festival. This stupa was built around the 5th-6th century and previously called Dharma Chakra. The stupa consists of a 28m diameter stone plinth which rises to a height of 13m. The upper part of this structure seems unfinished.*
Following pages 60-61: *The young and the old at Dhamek stupa, Sarnath. While the little boy sprints towards who knows what, there is an old believer who has stopped on his tracks to reiterate his faith.*

great concern with 'finding the self', a concern which preoccupied the teachers of that age.

At Uruvela, where he had earlier practised austerities, he now sought to win over the Kashyapa brothers and their very large following. To this end he is said to have performed many magical acts and gradually built up a good following. And thus with a fast expanding group the Buddha entered Rajgir.

Rajagriha or the present day Rajgir, then ruled by King Bimbisara became closely associated with the Buddha. In King Bimbisara, the Buddha found an influential patron. Bimbisara's son and successor Ajatasatru was initially no friend but later he too became a follower. Ajatasatru later erected a *stupa* over the relics of the Buddha. Other important disciples were: Sariputta, Mogallana, and Jivaka, physician to the king. A council was also held here during the following monsoon of BC 480 under Mahakashyapa after the death of the Buddha. At this First Council, the definite texts of the *Vinaya Pitaka*, edited by the Buddha's favourite disciple Ananda and Upali were accepted. They were recited in chorus by the five hundred monks who assembled there. Hence the assembly was called a *sangiti*, which means singing together.

Though Ajatasatru's successor Udayina moved the capital to Pataliputra, Rajgir continued to remain an important site visited by subsequent travellers. King Ashoka created a pillar to mark his visit. Fa Hsien worshipped, at the cave at 'Vulture Peak' and Hiuen Tsang has left a detailed account describing the *stupas* and monasteries, even though by the time he arrived they were beginning to wear a desolate and deserted look. Pataliputra was originally a village called Pataligama which the Buddha visited at the invitation of its people. Under Ajatasatru we hear of it being fortified by his ministers against the Vajjian confederacy. These ministers named two gates of the town after the Buddha. Not too far away was a village where the Buddha was staying, when the courtesan Ambapalli came to invite him to Vaishali. When the Buddha arrived in Rajgir it was initially thought that he was a disciple of Uruvela Kashyapa. Soon enough it came to be known that the Buddha was himself the teacher. King Bimbisara came to meet him and hear his sermon. Bimbisara became a patron and follower, the latter, when the Buddha allowed the *Sangha* to accept Bimbisara's gift of a *vihara* (a retreat for Buddhists). This served as an abode for the *Sangha* during the rainy season when the monks were forbidden to travel.

Orchards and graves became acceptable offerings to the *Sangha*. They provided convenient but secluded retreats. A gift provided the lay follower a way to gain merit but by itself a gift was insufficient: *dana* or gift offerings were only a means to merit. However, the Buddha is reported to have told the Licchavi general Siha that *dana* would lead to fame and even rebirth.

The conversion of Sariputta and Mogallana, who were pupils of the non-Brahmana teacher Sanjaya Belatthputta was an important event as was the conversion of Mahakashyapa. Alongwith these three major disciples many others sought refuge in the Buddha. In later traditions Sariputta came to represent wisdom while Mogallana stood for magical powers. Mahakashyapa was also, like the former two, a Brahmana and after the passing away of the Buddha he played a crucial role in preserving the original teachings of the Buddha.

The initial response to the message of the Buddha was not one of instant submission; many voices were raised against his ideas. He had to debate and argue, preach and exhort and patiently build up a following. Devadatta, the Buddha's infamous cousin, in part, represents a criticism of the Buddhist doctrine from the ascetic point of view, while others saw in the Buddha's

Image of Tibetan Buddha evidenced in ornate resplendence against an intricate backdrop, accompanied by little Buddhist idols.

The yellow Buddha here indicates the iconography which follows the Tibetan prescription for casting a sacred idol.

teaching of non-attachment a principle which would lead to the disruption of the social order. For the latter the Buddha was destroying the world of the householder and ultimately the basis of society. If everyone were to renounce the world, how would society continue? The world of the *bikkhu* stood in constant tension with and apart from the world of the *gihi*, the householder.

On the other hand, Devadatta's attempt to split the *Sangha* was on grounds of the Buddha's laxity concerning monastic discipline. Devadatta wanted a strict observance of monastic rules. He was against permanent residences for the monks, arguing that they must live in the forest, beg for alms and wear only cast-off rags. They must not, he argued, accept gifts. These, Devadatta felt, should be the minimum conditions for being a member of

the *Sangha*. The Buddha rejected these terms.

Meanwhile King Suddhodana, hearing of his son's 'Enlightenment' sent the Buddha's childhood friend Udayina to request him to return to his home and family. The Buddha had been away from his family for seven years. Finally, the Buddha returned to Kapilavastu. However, the return was far from joyous: traditional stories stress the tensions. The father is not yet fully reconciled to his son's 'homeless state', and finds his begging for alms unbecoming of a Sakya prince. But it was not Siddhartha who had returned. He had gone to Kapilavastu not as a son but as the Buddha, as the 'Enlightened One'.

Among the many stories it is perhaps the meeting with his son Rahula that most poignantly underlines this difference. Yasodhara, the forsaken wife of the

Buddha, hopes to win back the Siddhartha who had left her and she puts forth her son Rahula, hoping that his presence would perhaps influence his father. Rahula asks for his inheritance but the Buddha understands it to mean that he is looking for deliverance and consents to take him into the *Sangha*. In a similar manner the Buddha's half-brother Nanda is taken into the *Sangha* on the eve of his marriage and of his becoming the crown prince. Finally, five hundred Sakya princes come to have their heads shaved and enter the *Sangha*.

The story of the conversion of the Sakya princes has an important leitmotif: the equality of men. When the princes came to the Buddha's retreat they found that the barber Upali had already been ordained. The princes had to treat Upali as an equal, for the Law of the Buddha belongs equally to all. The idea that salvation was open to all, regardless of status or caste was an important element in Buddhist doctrine (although women and slaves were still treated as inferior). An illustrative story often quoted is that of the four birds, each of a different colour which fell at the feet of the Buddha and became white. Along with Upali, who went on to play a distinguished role in the *Sangha* and became the editor of the rules of monastic discipline, there were other converts from the lower castes. Yasoja, the fisherman, Ghatikara, the potter, and Suthadda, the barber were some of the better known monks from the low castes.

From Kapilavastu, the Buddha turned his attention to the powerful kingdom of Kosala, then ruled by King Pasenadi. This was one of the four powerful kingdoms which at the time of the Buddha controlled most of the middle Ganga plain. The Sakyas were actually subordinate to the Kosala kingdom which had its capital at Savatthi (or Sravasti), and the Buddha is said to have spent twenty-five rainy seasons, the period when travel was forbidden here

and consequently many of his sermons were delivered in this city.

The major events associated with this city are: the story of Anathapindika, the gift of the garden Jetavana, the debate with the Jainas and the *Ajivikas* and the faith of Visakha. Sravasti has been described by the later Chinese travellers, and here too the monasteries evidently lay in ruins in the growing wilderness. Today the site is known as Sahet-Mahet and it was the indefatigable Sir Alexander Cunningham who identified the location during his excavation here in 1863.

Sravasti, at the time of the Buddha was the centre of six non-Brahminical teachings, among whom the Jainas and the *Ajivikas* were most important. It is not unlikely that the Buddha came here to try and win adherents through debate and discussion. He chose to stay at the garden of Jetavana and preach to the royal family. King Pasenadi was a brother-in-law of King Suddhodana, but it was only gradually that he was won over by the Buddha. Initially a very ardent patron of the Buddha was the merchant Anathapindika. It was he who presented the garden of Jetavana, according to the stories, covering it with gold for the Buddha. Later he also built monasteries for the monks.

Another early adherent and lavish patron was Visakha, the wife of the merchant Punnavadhana and the daughter of the Sethi Saketa. She not only built a monastery but by her perseverance and display of devotion was able to convert her father-in-law, who was a Jaina, to the Buddhist persuasion.

The story is told that as King Pasenadi's admiration for the Buddha increased he decided to have a Hall of Law built. Here a great debate between the Buddha and the other teachers was to be held. The *Ajivikas* were represented by the teacher Makhali Gosala, who had a particularly strong following in this region. Vardhamana, the Jaina and Sanjaya, the former teacher of Sariputta and Mogallana also took part.

Buddhist pilgrims pay obeisance at the bodhi *tree site at Sravasti. They venerate a little statue of the Buddha at the foot of the tree.*

Later traditions hold that the Buddha, after preaching the Law, vanquished his opponents by a dazzling display of magic. The Buddha, it is said, caused a mango tree to grow from a seed to full height, flower and bear fruit. This, in a certain tradition, is called the 'Miracle of the Mango'. The miracle has been gracefully depicted on the north gate of the Sanchi stupa. There are other traditions which speak of water spirits bringing huge lotuses. Though it must be said that irrespective of these miracle-stories, it emerges clearly that argument and debate were an acceptable and commonly used form for arriving at the truth, at refining belief and winning adherents.

The Buddha, having won converts in Magadha, Kosala and his home town Kapilavastu, according to later tradition, ascended the heavens of the thirty-three gods to convert his mother, Queen Maya.

This was sixteen years after 'Enlightenment', during the period of rest in the three rainy months. He showed his mother, who had died seven days after his birth, the Law. Having assured her salvation he descended to the earth at Sankasya. At present this town is called Sankisa and even though it is in the middle of the Gangetic plain, it is far removed from other Buddhist sites.

The descent of the Buddha, also called the 'Miracle of Sankasya' is usually depicted in sculpture or painting with the Buddha escorted by Brahma on the right and Indra on the left. The triple staircase which they descend is depicted as built with jewels by the gods themselves. Emperor Ashoka is said to have built a stone copy of it which was seen by the Chinese travellers, Fa Hsien and Hiuen Tsang.

The stories which show the Buddha handling contentious monks or false

The scene of the worship of a modern image of the Buddha in Sarnath — the significance being that it represents the Buddha giving his first sermon which was delivered to five Sanghas.

Facing page: *Wall paintings from Sarnath (main temple). The* mise-en-scene *in this evokes the traditional story of the Buddha preaching a sermon to King Prasenjit after attaining supreme knowledge.*

implications are legion. That of the Brahmana, Bharadvaja is aptly illustrative. Bharadvaja lived near the city of Rajgir and one day he chanced upon the Buddha begging for alms. Bharadvaja, incensed, upbraided the Buddha, 'O wanderer, I too, plough and sow and so find my livelihood. Do you also plough and sow to the same end?' The Buddha, having faced such criticism replied with equanimity, 'I, too plough and sow, and it is thus that I find my food.' Bharadvaja was 'perplexed and enquired, 'I do not see, O revered Gautama, that you have a yoke, plough share, goad or bullocks. How, then, say that you too labour?' The Buddha calmly replied, 'Faith is the seeds I sow, devotion is the rain; modesty is the plough share and goad, energy is my team and bullock, leading to safety, and proceeding without backsliding to the place where there is no sorrow.' Bharadvaja was thus moved by this answer to acknowledge the superiority of the Buddha's teachings and he sought and obtained admission to the *Sangha.*

Where the Buddha Passed Away

*Through me shall the words be said
to make death exhilarating.
Nor will I allow you any more
to balk me with what I was calling life.*

—Walt Whitman

The final years of the Buddha's life are marked by the loss of close friends as well as contention within the *Sangha*. The political situation was changing; his two friends, King Bimbisara of Magadha and King Pasenadi of Kosala were murdered by their sons and their thrones usurped. Within the *Sangha* the Buddha's cousin Devadatta rose to challenge the Buddha, not just for the position of leadership but also to question his practices. The final years were spent, not in peace and contentment but in bringing the *Sangha* to order.

It was during the Buddha's visit to Kapilavastu that he had converted Devadatta, along with the other five hundred Sakya princes. Devadatta, in the later Buddhist texts, emerges as the schismatic who seeks domination. Although a brilliant and able man, he was unscrupulous and scheming: he wanted to succeed the Buddha, who was then seventy-two years old. The Buddha, however, refused. After him there would only be the Law and the *Sangha*. Devadatta, instead of submitting carried out a series of increasingly violent attempts to eliminate the Buddha and establish his supremacy. Some even impute Ajatasatru's killing of his father, King Bimbisara, to Devadatta's evil machinations. The attempts started with an attack on the Buddha's life by hired killers. Devadatta then

Facing page: An Ashoka Pillar situated in Vaishali and neighbouring Buddhist structures which attract pilgrims and tourists from several countries of South-East Asia. The pillar itself is built of highly polished red sandstone and is 18.3 m high with a life size lion carved on top. Ashokan Pillars, as such, have been erected in and mark places sanctified by the Buddha.

set the elephant Nalagiri (with the reputation for being a killer), loose on him. The charge of the elephant 'with trunk in the air, ears erect, and tail rigid', became a famous subject in Buddhist art. Later texts further embellish the scene: 'from the head of the Buddha sprang five lions which kept the elephant at bay.'

The struggle with Devadatta, when voided of mythical flourishes, is seen to be centred around the practices of the *Sangha*. Many monks had become critical of what they perceived as the laxity of the rules of the *Sangha*. Contention arose over the rules pertaining to residence, acceptance of invitations to dinner, clothing, shelter and food. Devadatta and others were critical of the Buddha for they found him wanting in the strict observance of ascetic discipline.

Devadatta advocated, as a minimum condition, strict observance of the rules—monks could eat only what they begged, robes could only be made from mended rags, there could be no permanent shelters, monks must abstain from eating meat and fish. It was at Vaishali that this controversy about the rules broke out and Devadatta, when his ideas were not accepted by the Buddha, left with five hundred monks. The size of the dissatisfied group shows that there were many monks who were happier following a path of severe denial and austerity and had not really come to terms with the Buddha's 'Middle Path'. Chinese travellers write of his group as a distinct order—these monks continued to venerate only the Buddha of the past. Thus Devadatta's group represents an early break within the *Sangha*.

Devadatta marks an early schism, a questioning of the philosophical and organizational principles around which the Buddha had built the *Sangha*. This challenge was successfully met, but another arose from the outside involving the kingdoms of Kosala and Magadha. The political situation began to change with the usurpation of the Kosala throne by Virudhaka, who drove his father, King Pasenadi out of the kingdom. The usurpation occurred, quite significantly, while

Pasenadi was visiting the Buddha. Virudhaka pursued a policy of expansion and extended the ambit of his control. He sought to subdue the proud Sakyas against whom, it is said, he had an old grudge. (The story is told that Virudhaka's mother, a Sakyan, was actually of low origin and the Sakyas had deliberately misled Pasenadi when he sought a Sakyan bride. Virudhaka, again according to tradition, died in a fire and went to hell in atonement of his sins.)

The neighbouring kingdom of Magadha was also ruled by a parricide, Ajatasatru, who was as much in the process of expanding his territories. Ajatasatru's physician Jivaka was a Buddhist and it is said that under his influence Ajatasatru sought to win the Buddha over by repenting the killing of his father. 'In my foolishness, in my blindness, in my wickedness I have caused my father's death, this virtuous man and virtuous king. May the blessed one, O lord, accept the confession of my sins so that I shall not sin again.'

In trying to expand his kingdom, Ajatasatru sought to conquer the Vajji confederacy which was a tribal grouping. He sent his minister, Varshakara to find out from the Buddha whether he would be able to successfully subdue the Vajjian confederacy or not. The Buddha was in his seventy-ninth year when the minister came. Instead of answering his question directly he turned to Ananda and defined the reasons for the Vajji strength. He said that the Vajji held frequent public meetings, lived peacefully, were respectful of the law, displayed respect for the aged and for women, were kind towards saints and venerated sanctuaries.

The Buddha, while supporting the republican system of the Vajjis, used this occasion to compare it with the *Sangha*. What he was saying was that the *Sangha* too could remain strong as long as it was united and in concord. He also stressed that the *bikkhus* should 'delight in a life of solitude . . . not engage in, be fond of, or be connected with business . . . should exercise themselves in mental activity, search after truth, energy, joy, peace, earnest contemplation and equanimity of mind . . . shall exercise themselves in the realisation of the ideas of the impermanency of all phenomena, bodily or mental, the absence of every soul . . . so long may the brethren be expected not to decline but to prosper.'

The rainy season came to an end and the monks were to go forth and preach the 'Law'. The Buddha too set out with Ananda and other monks from Rajgir, the Magadhan capital. He stopped briefly at Ambalathika, the mango tree nursery where he delivered a sermon. His next stop was Nalanda, the home of Sariputta. Nalanda later emerges as a great university around the 4th century AD, though Emperor Ashoka had built a monastery there earlier. Its period of glory was however during the rule of the imperial Guptas (5th century), one of whom, Narsimha Gupta, built a brick temple.

The Nalanda Mahavihara was, according to the Chinese traveller Hiuen Tsang, built on a mango garden donated by a rich merchant. He describes the place as being remarkable for grandeur and height: 'The richly adorned towers and the fairy-like turrets, like pointed hill tops, are congregated together. The observatories seem to be lost in the vapour of the morning, and the upper rooms tower above the clouds.' This magnificent structure was surrounded by translucent pools and had 'roofs covered with tiles that reflect the light in a thousand shades.'

At this university, ten thousand scholars are said to have resided and there were over a thousand teachers. They were all fed and clothed free. Each, according to Hiuen Tsang, received daily 'one hundred and twenty *janbiras* (a fruit), twenty areca nuts, twenty nutmegs, an ounce of camphor, and a pick of the finest variety of rice called Mahasali which grew only in Magadha and every month three measures of oil and a daily supply of butter, etc. Each resident was further provided with two servants and one elephant.'

The monastery, with the lands given to it which were cultivated by its residents managed to support itself. Gradually the monastery acquired police as well as administrative rights.

The site of temple no. 2 at Nalanda Vihar, where one of the earliest universities was founded. Hiuen Tsang, the Chinese traveller, thought that the name 'Nalanda', which means charity without intermission, derives from the Buddha's liberality, or generosity in a previous birth. Nalanda experienced one of the strongest monastic movements after the Buddha's passing away.

In the 7th century, when Hiuen Tsang came, over a hundred villages were endowed to the Nalanda monastery and later their number was increased to two hundred.

During the Buddha's time, the teacher himself was the institution and monasteries were meant for monks and nuns. Gradually, corporate centres of education came up. Early medieval temple colleges at Salolgi, Eunariram, Tirumukudda are such examples. Nalanda remained a flourishing centre till the 12th century when Bakhtiyar Khalji destroyed it. It is said that it took six months to burn. It was Alexander Cunningham who identified the modern Bargaon with Nalanda in 1871 but it was only in 1915 that systematic excavations were undertaken.

From Nalanda, the Buddha proceeded to Pataligrama on the Ganga, where the great Mauryan rulers later built their capital and which today is Patna. Here he observed the preparations being carried out by Ajatasatru's ministers: forts being built against the Licchavis. With the rainy season upon them, the Buddha and his monks reached Vaishali. Here he stopped with his disciple Ananda at Beluva, the bamboo village (in the vicinity of Kushinagara).

Vaishali, capital of the powerful Licchavis, is also closely associated with the Buddha. The two most striking incidents here are the stories of the courtesan, Ambapalli and the Buddha's foster mother, Mahaprajapati.

The Buddha, much to the discomfiture of the Licchavi nobles, accepted an invitation for a meal from Ambapalli. The Licchavi nobles begged and pleaded with her and offered to recompense her if she would withdraw the invitation but she was adamant and the Buddha, who believed in equality of all,

Old stupa, *Kushinagara. The* stupa *originally was a funerary structure serving to protect the holy relics of the Buddha or other saints. Most of these were prominent burial mounds protected maybe with brickworks.*

dined with her. Mahaprajapati was an aunt of the Buddha who had acted as his foster mother after the death of Queen Maya. When the Buddha came to Kapilavastu she had tried unsuccessfully to join the *Sangha*. In spite of the Buddha's refusal she continued to persevere and arrived in Vaishali bedraggled, footsore and weary. The Buddha remained reluctant to allow her to join but with the support of Ananda she ultimately convinced him. She founded the *Bikkuni Sangha* or the order of nuns.

Both the stories are illustrative of the changing attitudes towards women. The growth of a sophisticated urban culture is apparent with the existence of courtesans like Ambapalli. At the same time she did not acquire social status, for such practices were not universally accepted. The Brahmanas were opposed to them. For instance, a Brahmana would not take food offered by a *ganika* or prostitute. On the other hand, the Buddha by

accepting Ambapalli's invitation displayed a tolerant attitude. He was treating her as a socially acceptable individual. Yet, his reluctance to allow women into the order does reflect that the change was one of degree. While Ananda's insistence gained Mahaprajapati's ordination, nuns still had to be reborn as men to gain salvation.

At Beluva, the Buddha became violently ill, an illness which would finally claim his life. It was here that he delivered his final sermon and explained his views about the *Sangha*. It is said that Ananda asked him for instructions but the Buddha refused, saying, 'now the *Tathagata*, Ananda, thinks not that it is he who should lead the brotherhood, or that the order is dependent on him. Why then should he leave instructions in any matter concerning the Order?' He went on to add, 'Therefore, O, Ananda, be ye lamps unto yourselves. Be ye a refuge to yourselves. Betake yourselves to no external refuge. Hold fast to the truth as a lamp!'

New stupa, *Kushinagara. With passage of time,* stupa *architecture has evolved a complex design symbolically representing the cosmos in an elementary form (module): the square base (earth), the sphere (air), the triangular upthrust (flame), the crescent (water), the conical drop (ether).*

The Buddha recovered for a while but the end was near. He made frequent trips to Vaishali, the city he loved. It is said that when he set out for home he said, 'It is the last time O, Ananda, that the "Predestined One" looks upon Vaishali, he will never return!' The Licchavis are said to have built a *stupa* to commemorate that event, after they brought their share of the Buddha's relics. Later Chinese travellers describe the *stupa*, but by the time of Hiuen Tsang the city was in ruins, though the stupa and an Ashokan pillar still existed. Hiuen Tsang also describes a stone tank reportedly dug up by a group of monkeys. As with other sites, Vaishali lay in obscurity till located by Alexander Cunningham. He identified it with the present town of Basrah in the district of Muzaffarpur, Bihar.

Later tradition relates that the Buddha, before setting out on his final journey, asked Ananda whether he should live on for another *kalpa* (a whole age, from creation to final dissolution) but Ananda remained silent. Another story narrates Mara's visit to the Buddha, who finally agreed to seek *pari-nibbana*. (death or the cessation of being). Regardless of these stories it is clear that the Buddha set out from Vaishali towards Kapilavastu but he was not fated to reach his destination. After Vaishali he stopped briefly at Pava. Here the Buddha rested at the mango orchard of Kunda, the blacksmith's son. It is here that he is supposed to have eaten a meal which infected his stomach and led to intense dysentery which caused his death. In the later tradition, to absolve Kunda of any blame, he tells Ananda, 'There are two offerings of food of equal merit and equal fruitfulness, more meritorious and profitable than any other: the one eaten by the "Predestined One" before the supreme and perfect "Enlightenment" and the one eaten by

73

A modern Buddha idol in Rajgir, with the mudra *(hand posture) representing the gesture of sermon.*

the "Predestined One" before his final decease.'

Kunda's offering is obviously a later addition and complements Sujata's earlier offering. The acts of the divine Buddha thus attain the shape of a predestined sequence. The Buddha, debilitated by attacks of dysentery, was weak and weary and had to stop mid-way at Kushinagara. At a stream, Kakuttha, the Buddha drank water, muddied by the passing of a large caravan, much against the advice of Ananda. Here while the Buddha was resting, Putkasa, a noble of the Malla clan which ruled Kushinagara, came by and engaged him in discussion. This noble had studied under Arada Kalpa, under whom the Buddha too had studied for a while. The noble was awed by the Buddha and presented him a cloth 'the colour of gold, shining and ready to wear'. It is said that when Ananda clothed the Buddha with this cloth, it lost its lustre because of the greater brilliance emanating from the Buddha.

The Buddha continued his painful journey. Crossing the river Hiranyavati, he rested in a *sal* grove of the Mallas. To Ananda he said, 'Come Ananda, spread for me a couch with its head to the north between the twin *sal* trees. I am weary, Ananda and would lie down . . .' and the 'Blessed One' laid himself down on his right side, with one leg resting on the other and he was totally and self-possessed. At the third watch, in the *sal* grove, the Buddha attained the Great Departure or Decease, *Mahaparinibbana.*

This *sal* grove where the Buddha attained the Great Departure or Decease was in Kushinagara in Nepal. While some excavations had been carried out earlier it was during 1861-2 that Alexander Cunningham identified the site. Later, the well-known *nibbana* statue of the Buddha was uncovered as well as other structures. As with the other sites, both Ashoka and the Chinese travellers had visited them. Hiuen Tsang wrote, 'He is lying with his head to the north as if asleep. By the side

The sleeping Buddha, in a position of recline, one which corresponds with the salvational 'posture'—a part of the Shanti Stupa ensemble at Rajgir.

of this *vihara* is a stupa built by King Ashoka. Before it is a stone pillar which records the *nirvana* of the *Tathagata*.'

When the Buddha was near his end, Ananda said, 'Let not the Blessed One die in this little wattle and daub town in the midst of a jungle.' The Buddha replied that it was a large and prosperous city with a great and virtuous ruler. In his last hours the Buddha made arrangements for his end. He first consoled the dejected Ananda by telling him that it was in the nature of things that 'we must divide ourselves from them, leave them, sever ourselves from them.' Ananda was then sent to inform the Mallas of the approaching demise of the Buddha so that they could come and pay their respects. Before his end the Buddha was to convert one more person: a man, Subhadra, full of doubts came to him seeking clarification, searching for answers. Ananda tried to turn Subhadra away but the Buddha called the man back and taught him.

Subhadra's doubts were dispelled and he was converted and even ordained. He was the last disciple converted by the Buddha.

Before the Buddha went into those successive stages of meditation where sensation and ideas cease to exist, he gave his final exhortation: 'Behold now, brethren, I exhort you, saying: decay is inherent in all composite things! Work out your salvation with diligence.' Later traditions made out the funeral of Buddha to be a grand affair, much as it would have been for a *Chakravartin Raja*, a universal monarch. With his passing away his relics were divided into eight parts and carried away by the faithful.

***Following pages 76-77:** The great scene of the Buddha's* Mahaparinirvana *from Kushinagara.* Mahaparinirvana, *the great departing is a major event that the Buddhist iconography commemorates. The story goes that the Buddha fell seriously ill at Kushinagara (in Nepal) and 'passed away' in the shadow of a* sal *grove.*

Places of Buddhist Interest

Ajanta Caves (Maharashtra) — near the city of Aurangabad, contain masterpieces (drawings and murals) on the life-story of the Buddha and

An Ajanta mural of the 6th-7th century.

also feature *Jataka* stories on the Buddha's previous births. Both early Hinayana and the latter Mahayana creations are included here. These are singularly Buddhist caves unlike the nearby Ellora with Hindu, Jain and Buddhist caves.

Amaravati (Andhra Pradesh) — 35 km north of Guntur, was a great Mahayana Buddhist centre. The Great Stupa here whose origins go back to the 3rd - 2nd centuries BC, was believed to have been 32 m in height and diameter, larger than Sanchi. The Archaeological Museum here contains panels, railings and sculptures of the *bodhi* tree, *chakras* and caskets containing relics.

Dharamsala (Himachal Pradesh) — a hill station mainly identified with Dalai Lama and the Tibetan community in exile. Hosts the Namgyal Monastery at McLeodganj, the upper part of the town, with the Centre of Tibetan Studies with one of the best libraries for studying Tibet's Buddhist culture. Among other places of interest here: Norbulingka Institute, a major centre of Buddhist teaching and the Tushita Meditation Centre.

Dharmsala is identified with Dalai Lama, the spiritual leader of the exiled Tibetans.

Karli (or Karla) and Bhaja Caves (near Bombay) — Karli has the largest Buddhist *chaitya* or chapel cave in India, which dates from the 2nd-1st century BC. And the Bhaja caves dating from the 2nd century BC, include the first apsidal *chaitya* (a long hall with a semi-circular end).

The old Kharding Monastery (Himachal Pradesh) — at Lahaul was the former capital of this region and overlooks Keylong town. People in this region follow a Tibetan form of Tantric Buddhism with a panoply of demons, saints and followers.

Tibetan stupas or chortens at Ladakh.

Ladakh — this high-altitude Himalayan plateau, almost exclusively Buddhist in religion and culture has the Red (Tsempo) *gompa* (local name for monastery) built in AD 1430, at Leh, the region's capital. This *gompa* contains a fine three-storey-high seated

Buddha image. In addition, there are massive Buddha statues at Alchi and at the Basgo *gompa*, figures of the Buddha.

Nagarjunakonda (Andhra Pradesh) — is a valley with one of the richest Buddhist sites. The valley hosts around thirty Buddhist buildings (several small and big *stupas*) of Hinayana and Mahayana Buddhism. The striking development here was the changing of the wheel shaped *stupa* (a Buddhist symbol) into an architectural plan.

Giant Buddha statue at Dhauli.

Dhauli (Orissa) — was where the horrors of the Kalinga war led King Ashoka to be converted to Buddhist teachings. Two Ashokan edicts are to be found here called the 'Kalinga Edicts'. Also, there exists here on a hill-top the 'Peace Pagoda' built by the Japan Buddha Sangha in early 1970s.

Rumtek Monastery (Sikkim) — is the main centre of Kagyu ('black hat') order of Tibetan Lamaistic Buddhism and possesses statues, *thangkas* and scriptures. At Gangtok, the state capital, exists the Research Institute of Tibetology to spur research on Mahayana Buddhism. The library here has fine *thangkas* and icons.

Sanchi (Madhya Pradesh) — 46 km north of Bhopal, has the oldest Buddhist structures (with carvings in yellow sandstone), even if without any apparent link to the Buddha's life. Extraordinary places of interest here: the Great Stupa, originally built by Emperor Ashoka in 3rd century BC and the *toranas*, which are four gateways containing scenes from the Buddha's life carved on the surrounding pillars and also from legends from the *Jataka* stories. The Archaeological Museum here contains findings from the Ashokan period (caskets, pottery, parts of gateway, images).

One of the four gateways, or toranas *at Sanchi.*

Tabo Gompa (Spiti, Himachal Pradesh) — is considered one of the most important monasteries of the Lamaistic persuasion. Its colourful wall paintings are comparable to Ajanta murals. The *gompa* enjoys a collection of *thangkas*, scriptures and art pieces. These last include clay images of the Buddha in a myriad poses.

Images associated with the Buddha at Tabo monastery.

Udayagiri and Khandagiri Caves (Orissa) — near Bhubaneshwar, these caves with friezes, figures and motifs testify to the Buddhist and Jaina influence in this region around the 2nd century BC.

First Published 1997
Reprinted in 1999
© Lustre Press Pvt. Ltd. 1997
M-75, Greater Kailash-II Market,
New Delhi-110 048, INDIA
Phones: (011) 6442271, 6462782, 6460886
Fax: (011) 6467185, 6213978
E-mail: rolibook@del2.vsnl.net.in

ISBN: 81-7437-086-2

Typesetting: Naresh L. Mondal
Production: Naresh Nigam, Abhijit Raha
Concept & Design: Roli CAD Centre

Photo Credits:

Aditya Arya
Bindu Arora
J. L. Nou
Pramod Kapoor
Sondeep Shankar
Taj Mohammad
Lustre Press Library

Fotomedia:

Aditya Arya
Ajay Sud
Ananta Padmanabha Rao
Ashok Dilwali
B.P.S. Walia
D. Nayak
Francois Gautier
Jyoti Banerjee
Mahantesh Morabad
P.K. De
Prem Kapoor
Ram Krishna Sharma

*The publishers express their grateful thanks for the help
rendered by Dr Pushpesh Pant and Dr Moonis Joshi.*

Printed and bound in Singapore